T0061566

Introduction

One hundred years ago, Coco Chanel was redefining how women dressed. Her affinity with menswear, desire to liberate women from the constricts of corsets and sense of spare elegance marked a total sea change in style, one which continues to reverberate all these years later. Aside from her signatures – the LBD, the quilted 2.55 bag and two-tone shoes – it was her attitude to clothes and their power which has endured. True, she had an extraordinary life, beginning as an orphan raised in a convent and becoming the world's most wealthy woman. Trailblazer, provocateur, businesswoman extraordinaire – Coco had it all. But her mystique was always as much about her wit as her wardrobe and the advice she offered women on style, beauty and confidence continues to resonate in countless ways.

This book is a modern reimagining of 30 of her iconic quotes, bringing Coco's advice right up to date. We hope that her timeless guidance will help you add that pinch of *je ne sais quoi* every single day.

COCO
rules

LOM
ART

Contents

1

Every colour in the rainbow suits you

Once upon a time, women were issued diktats about which shades flattered their colouring. Were you a 'winter' or more of a 'spring'? After your shades were determined, you were free to enter the world of fashion, so long as you stuck to your colour prescription. Ever the rule-breaker, Coco always encouraged a liberating rebellion against these arbitrary judgements. Her attitude was that the hue which looks good on you is the one that makes you feel your most vibrant. Perhaps the colour experts might disagree, but the colour of confidence never goes out of style.

How many of us have felt embarrassed to wear red lipstick? Or suffered the jitter of nerves when debuting a shocking pink cocktail dress or an ochre velvet suit? Vivid colour can be intimidating, but it projects absolute self-assurance, something which is incredibly valuable if you're hoping to stand out – whether for business or personal reasons. There's also a spectrum of easy-to-wear shades, from claret to forest green, which inject personality without drawing so much spotlight. No matter which pigment you pick – even if your signature is head to toe black – channel Coco's self-belief and own the room, no matter what colour you choose.

Not quite ready to embrace those shockingly bold shades?

Swap them for a more muted counterpart.

Instead of ...	*You could try ...*
Shocking pink	Rose or salmon
Blood red	Claret, brick or mahogany
Emerald	Forest green, sage or olive

Alternatively, try a print in a bold hue as a less daunting alternative to block colour.

THE BEST COLOUR IN THE WHOLE WORLD IS THE ONE THAT LOOKS GOOD ON YOU.

2

You're a one-off, quit trying to change yourself to look like someone else

When it comes to our looks, the grass is always greener. If your style is classic, sophisticated and elegant, you may yearn for a modern and edgy aesthetic. If your figure resembles a beanpole, you may dream of Rubenesque curves, and vice versa. It's incredibly easy to become fixated on what you don't have when we are bombarded with images of aspirational beauty, and a perceived shortfall can make you feel you're in some way lacking. Being inspired by someone else's looks can be an act of self-expression and affinity. But, holding them up as the standard of beauty and copying their style stitch for stitch could make you forget your own matchless appeal.

That doesn't mean there is any one style which fits a certain shape, or any look that should be forbidden for a certain age. It's the way the clothing makes you feel, and if that isn't confident, don't waste your time. If a style or trend doesn't suit you or make you feel wonderful, move on quickly.

How to shop for your own fashion identity

• When you're trying on a new outfit, always ask yourself, does this feel like me or am I trying to look like someone else?

• In order to get a clear picture of what the 'you' looks like, scan through your favourite wardrobe ensembles. Is there something that links them together? Colour? Print? A certain kind of cut or attitude? Are you minimal, or glamorous? If your go-to look reflects a decade, which is it?

• While it's always fun to mix it up, and obviously our taste evolves over time, trying to find a connection to your quintessential style personality will increase the likelihood that you will wear your new purchase time and time again.

DON'T SPEND TIME BEATING ON A WALL, HOPING TO TRANSFORM IT INTO A DOOR.

3

Basics don't have to be boring

Fussy, overwrought outfits were Coco's nightmare –
but her design discipline wasn't about stripping away,
instead it was always far more focused on the freedom
that simple wardrobe staples could offer women.
What Coco pioneered was a way of dressing
that didn't require endless amounts of
thought and time. A well-cut pair of black
trousers, paired with a nude or white
knit and easy to wear ballet pumps will
never, ever fall out of style,
whereas tulle frills and
ruffles will come and go.

Coco loved Breton stripes, oversized fisherman's knits, jersey and pearls and rarely strayed too far from her uniform. She also believed that women had far more important things to do than grapple with what to wear. Amen to that. From the very birth of her label, Coco's collections brought a new sense of ease, and instead of the garters and gussets that had come before, Coco favoured clean lines and a mix-and-match, muted palette of black, white and beige. Her iconic pieces, including the little black dress, tweed suits with four pockets and the 2.55 quilted bag are all uncomplicated, throw-on classics. Budget-appropriate versions of these basics still offer us straightforward style solutions today. The moral: simple is always effective.

Coco's staples for wardrobe simplicity

Cigarette pants: dressed up or down, they're always comfortable and always chic.

Chunky boots: toughen up a tea dress or combine with your favourite denim to stomp the streets.

Striped tee: Coco was the first to champion jersey for outerwear as well as underwear.

Leather bag: wear cross-body for practicality as well as style.

Classic coat: be it a trench, a pea coat or full-length cashmere, a well-fitting coat will look great for a lifetime.

"

**SIMPLICITY
IS THE
KEYNOTE
OF ALL TRUE
ELEGANCE.**

"

4

A signature lip colour can lift your mood as well as your look

Coco never left the house without her finishing swish of lip colour, so if you're feeling lacklustre, it might be worth following her lead. Launching Chanel's first lipstick collection of velvety shades in 1924, Coco also created her own bespoke crimson tone which became a signature throughout her life. While some might find red lipstick a little OTT for every day, the uplifting power of colour can't be doubted. The right shade can warm the skin, add drama, or simply inject polish. For low-key occasions or downtime, a warm matt brown or sheer plum tint are universally flattering, but if you really need a pep up, nothing beats a pop of bright red.

Discovering your own signature lip shade gives you a little bullet of confidence which you can slick across your lips in seconds to add personality and panache to whatever else you're wearing. The key is to keep experimenting and to never discount a new tone just because you thought a certain colour didn't suit you in the past – you might find that a summer glow or different outfit completely changes the game.

Match your shade to the occasion

Every day: matt warm brown, sheer plum, pinky nudes.

Office: lip tints, balms and shades that are easy to apply and layer.

Evening: statement red (compare plummy reds and orange reds to find your ideal shade).

" IF YOU'RE SAD, ADD MORE LIPSTICK AND ATTACK. "

5

Take inspiration from the catwalk but make designer trends your own

Fashionistas have a certain 'you can't sit with us' reputation, which can make the world of catwalks and champagne after-parties seem intimidating. But true fashion doesn't necessarily come from the page of a designer's sketchbook. Street style is what creates today's language of cool and the best thing about it is that anyone and everyone can get involved.

These days you don't need to be a supermodel or an A-list celebrity to start a trend, so how do you go about making your own street-style statement? You can start by looking to the runways for inspiration on the season's best new looks, then adapt them to suit your own tastes and budget. And remember, you don't need a fashion designer or influencer's seal of approval to wear something you love – according to Coco, true style has always been democratic.

How to do trends ... your way

• Love the latest colour trends, but not so keen on the styles you see on the store rails? Hunt in vintage shops and on designer resale sites instead, where you'll find dresses and trousers in every colour of the rainbow, perfect for creating your personal take on the designer palette.

• Whenever you go on holiday, check out the local markets for little wardrobe trinkets and unusual additions to your look. So many designers seek inspiration from their travels, and you'll be bound to find a totally unique take on a current trend.

• Try wearing everyday pieces in an unusual way: a cardigan back to front, oversize jeans slung super low or utilitarian footwear with elegant evening dresses. Trends often come from unexpected juxtapositions.

A FASHION THAT DOES NOT REACH THE STREETS IS NOT A FASHION.

6

Personal style doesn't have a price tag

In the age of Instagram and throwaway fashion, it can be easy to fall into the trap of believing you can't wear the same clothes twice. In stark contrast, Coco was a serial outfit repeater and wore her 'old as new' attitude as a badge of honour, because she believed in the power of perfectly cut, timeless classics that could be worn for years. Being more Coco means getting more style mileage out of what you already own.

While the newest, shiniest styles on the block can be seductive, sticking to your guns and not feeling the pressure to wear every trend under the sun are the first steps to creating your own personal style. While it's always fun to try out something different, the outfit that fits you perfectly and brings back happy memories will always suit you far better than another box-fresh look that you've added to your basket on a whim. So next time you feel like you have nothing to wear, try shopping your closet before you make the splurge.

How to shop your closet

• Try everything on and package up for donation anything that doesn't fit, is worn out or that you simply don't love any more.

• Store clothes that are out of season or that you are keeping for sentimental reasons – they get in the way when you're dressing every morning.

• If you have some gems that you haven't worn for ages because they need tailoring or dry cleaning, make that a priority.

• Keep a list of pieces that make you feel great, so when you have an occasion or are packing for a trip you have a cheat sheet for reference.

ELEGANCE
DOES NOT
CONSIST IN
PUTTING
ON A NEW
DRESS.

Sleek and chic, black will never go out of style

Before Coco, black was worn mainly by women in mourning and young, working class 'shopgirls'. After Coco, black became the chicest (non) colour on the block. While every season heralds a 'new black', the truth is that nothing compares with the timeless, flattering, goes-with-everything appeal of the darkest shade. Whether you pair it with white or a neutral for monochromatic simplicity, with navy for a more modern tonal blend or leopard, polka or striped prints for a graphic 60s inspired look, black is a fail-safe.

Of course, head to toe black was Coco's favourite, and the appeal of a wardrobe in which every piece works seamlessly with each other cannot be overstated. The key to buying black is to focus on the design details, quality and the fit. Black can make you fade into the background – it's the opposite of a look-at-me colour. So, to make sure your outfit doesn't turn you into a wallflower, choose pieces with an interesting cut, which have been beautifully finished at the hems, sleeves and fastenings and fit you well. Remember there is black and then there is black – the memorable, stand-out-for-all-the-right-reasons black which Coco is famous for.

Which look are you?

Black+Leopard: glamorous, evening-ready with a retro twist.

Black+White: timeless monochrome, Mod-era chic, ageless.

Black+Navy: modern uniform, understated, great for the office.

Black+Black: creative, accomplished, quiet confidence.

Black+Spots: fun, feminine classic, ideal for date night.

WHEN I FIND A COLOUR DARKER THAN BLACK, I'LL WEAR IT. BUT UNTIL THEN, I'M WEARING BLACK!

99

8

Beauty comes in all shapes and sizes

What do you see when you look in the mirror? Is it a set of features and a hairstyle or the full, wonderfully multifaceted person that you are? The phrase 'beauty comes from within' has become hackneyed, but it's no less true today than when it was first written.

Beauty is about radiance, vivacity and self-possession, all by-products of happiness and being entirely at ease with yourself. When you can let go of comparisons to others and embrace the contours of your own face and body, you'll find yourself imbued with a particular kind of inner beauty. So, how do you get there? It's obviously easier said than done, but releasing a lot of messages you've internalized from a culture which promotes a uniform vision of beauty is a great start. No matter what your colouring, the angle of your nose or the shape of your body, no single 'type' has a monopoly on beauty and taking that on board is the first step. For too long, our definitions of beauty have been based on patriarchal, ageist, heteronormative and racist principles and too many have felt sub-standard or unworthy because of that.

Three steps to find your inner beauty

1. Stop editing your images
With the technology to alter your looks at your fingertips, it can be incredibly tempting to make tweaks here and there to tally with traditional beauty standards. Don't do it. Not only will it undermine your confidence, it further perpetuates the idea to other people that those standards mean something.

2. Broaden your beauty consumption
Audit the kinds of beauty you are consuming. Are you only reading magazines or watching films which feature a certain kind of look? Do you only follow people who look a certain way on social media? If so, take stock and add some more diverse types of beauty to the media you consume.

3. Self-care your way to beauty
Rather than undergoing expensive cosmetic treatments, invest time and energy in youself, be that through exercise, invigorating skin brushing, tactile moisturizing, cooking yourself delicious and nourishing food or restorative meditation. Looking after yourself isn't just an indulgence, it's a necessity.

" BEAUTY BEGINS THE MOMENT YOU DECIDE TO BE YOURSELF.

"

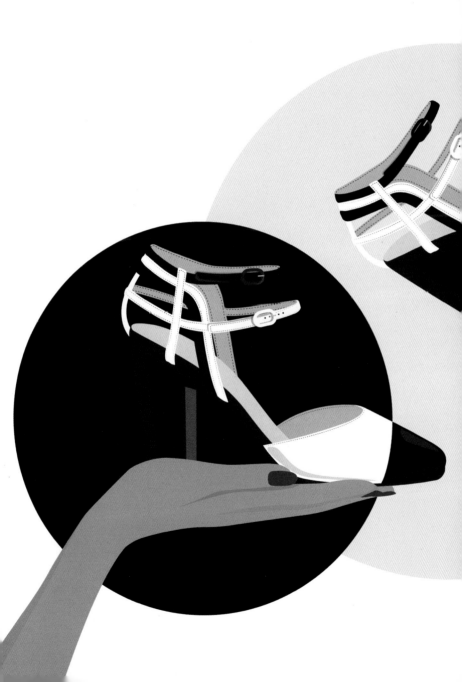

9

High heels are a good idea – but only if you can walk in them

Best known for her two-tone court shoes which feature a flattering combination of a black toe cap and pale-toned upper, Coco always favoured styles which were comfortable – famously wearing hers to play sports. So, heels should be high, yes, but never so tall that they interfere with anything that brings you joy.

While they may be a symbol of classic femininity, there's nothing less chic than not being able to move naturally in your footwear. The secret is that you only need a little height to lift your look. A one-inch pair of heels which you can sashay down the road comfortably in are far more flattering than towering stilettos which look good in a store but instantly turn you into Bambi. Coco always believed that fashion could act as a prop to help you build your self-esteem and that's exactly the transformative value that heels bring. As they require no small amount of effort, they express what you believe you deserve: high heels = high standards

Glossary of heels

Kitten heel: typically, one to two inches in height and often found on backless slip-ons or slingback styles.

Stiletto: the quintessential high heel, with a spindly heel of up to five inches high. While any style of shoe can have a stiletto heel, they're most associated with the stiletto close toe pump style.

Block heel: a thick heel of two inches and above, a block heel is often made of wood. Popularized in the 70s.

Platform: the heel is paired with a raised platform on the front part of the sole, offering a lift in height.

Flatform: a flat platform sole which raises the whole foot, rather than angling it like a traditional heel.

Wedge: a platform without a gap between the front sole and heel – one long wedge to create balance as well as height.

KEEP YOUR HEELS, HEAD AND STANDARDS HIGH.

10

Flaunt your flaws and you'll always be unforgettable

There are bound to be elements of your appearance which you're not 100% happy with. While beauty is, of course, in the eye of the beholder and there is no one standard of physical perfection, each of us have our own insecurities, however insignificant they may seem to everyone else. What Coco cottoned on to was that rather than needing to be concealed or covered up, these perceived 'flaws' are often where our individuality lies. Anything you might consider an imperfection adds to your charisma, and rather than seeing it as a blemish you should aim to recognize its charm.

Are there parts of your face or body that you spend time trying to hide? If so, it might be worth reappraising their value. Your natural quirks and unique features are what make you memorable, just like a one-off dress or limited-edition bag. Trying to airbrush them only makes you blend in, rather than Coco's advice which celebrates those unique qualities.

Flawed or fabulous?

It's worth remembering that 'flaws' are subjective and ever-changing. Some features, once considered imperfections, are now celebrated for their beauty, and vice versa:

A gap between your front teeth: considered a mark of beauty in medieval times and more recently welcomed as a dose of individuality in a sea of white veneers, celebrate the quirkiness of gapped 'dents du bonheur', the French phrase translating literally to 'lucky teeth'.

Freckled skin: for centuries, women have attempted to cover up freckles in pursuit of 'flawless' skin. But today, we are beginning to see freckles for what they are: totally unique, just like snowflakes for the skin.

Grey hair: once railed against as an incontrovertible sign of ageing, there is an ever-growing movement of people embracing silver tones, both natural and from a box.

WOMEN HIDE THEIR IMPERFECTIONS INSTEAD OF ACCEPTING THEM AS AN ADDED CHARM.

11

Underplay the dress code, no matter what the occasion

Coco always understood the power of nonchalance; the studied art of not caring too much. Being slightly underdressed is a shorthand way of communicating effortlessness, a fundamental part of elegance à la Chanel.

Translated, this means pitching your dress code just below what everyone else will be wearing. Black tie? Mix things up with a Le Smoking tuxedo and stilettos instead of a floor length gown. Smart/casual? Lean into the casual and pair tailored jeans and T-shirt with a boucle jacket and a piece of statement jewellery. For Cocktail, go va va voom with the dress, but muss up your hair and smudge your smoky eyeshadow to counteract the polish.

A word of caution here. While it is certainly chic to go low-key, you don't want to underdress so far that you a) feel drab or b) like you've just rolled out of bed and dressed in your floor-drobe. That's just rude.

How to dress down and add insouciance

If you've not got time to make it home from the office before heading out, never despair. Consider:

• Removing your shirt and wearing your suit buttoned up.

• Adding sneakers (think box-fresh white, rather than greying gym shoes).

• Undoing the top buttons of your shirt and adding a silk scarf knotted loosely like a necklace.

• Applying a smudgy eyeshadow to relax your makeup look instantly.

" IT IS ALWAYS BETTER TO BE SLIGHTLY UNDERDRESSED. "

12

It's not just about the clothes

Whenever you ask a designer where their inspiration comes from they will tell you the same thing: everywhere. The zeitgeist travels by osmosis, slowly infiltrating your tastes and desires until you no longer want those super-skinny jeans and you simply must have a pair of wide-leg kick flares. Fashion is often chided for being superficial and materialistic, but it is always a reflection of the times. The recent interest and investment in sustainability is an example of how fashion can encompass new attitudes and new ways of living in a positive way.

As a barometer, fashion can mirror all sorts of contemporary issues from boom-and-bust economies (the 'hemline index' suggest skirts get longer in recessions) through to shifting social values. Whether you wear androgynous, non-binary clothing, choose vegan leather or support brands disrupting the supply chain, fashion can be about so much more than the new-collar shape.

Let fashion reflect your ideas

Sustainability: the slow fashion movement (buying pieces made to last and re-wearing your favourites year after year) is something that Coco would certainly have endorsed. Throwaway fashion has never been chic.

La Garçonne: gender fluidity has caused a broad shift in thinking at many design houses and it's never been easier to mix and match between men's and women's collections – something which Coco pioneered all those decades ago. Shirts, denim and jersey are a great way to go if this strikes a chord with you.

FASHION IS IN THE SKY, IN THE STREET, FASHION HAS TO DO WITH IDEAS, THE WAY WE LIVE, WHAT IS HAPPENING.

99

13

Accessories can make and break any outfit

While she didn't coin it, Coco's style philosophy slots firmly into the 'less is more' camp. But that certainly doesn't mean that she didn't love adornment – her costume jewellery, brooches and endless strings of pearls prove she had a magpie-like eye for decoration. However, as with everything, Coco understood the power of balance. Too many trinkets can actually reduce the impact of a carefully considered outfit, while too few means you miss out on the final finishing touch.

Her advice is priceless, because who hasn't been there? It's so easy to get carried away with accessories, especially if you're in a rush and don't give yourself the once-over before you leave the house. Clean hair, a spritz of perfume and one piece of jewellery is all you really need to look pulled together, so if you do catch yourself wearing the hat, the glasses, the lipstick, the necklaces, the brooch, the earrings and bracelets too, you may have veered into fancy dress territory. But have no fear, as Coco says, all you need to do is ditch one or two pieces and you'll be back to stylish in a flash.

How to layer jewellery without going OTT

Layering jewellery can look great, but knowing where to stop is key to making the look work for you.

• With necklaces, choose different chain lengths and keep your pieces fine. Three heavy, beaded necklaces will overpower your outfit, whereas three glinting chains, ie: one choker length, one clavicle length and one chest length, will look elegant and bring a bohemian flavour to your ensemble.

• With bracelets, choose only one wrist to stack bangles on and leave the other one naked or with a simple watch to create an interesting asymmetry.

• Consider stacking multiple rings on one finger rather than wearing one on each digit. An usual pinkie or thumb ring can add some individuality.

BEFORE YOU LEAVE THE HOUSE, LOOK IN THE MIRROR AND TAKE ONE THING OFF.

14

Look outwards as well as inwards

The most exquisitely put together person will become immediately unattractive if you overhear them being rude to a waiter. There is absolutely no point being wonderfully clad if you behave appallingly – nothing ruins a look quicker than unkindness. Of course, being beautiful inside takes a lot more work than a slick of lipstick, and no-one is perfect. But if you're looking to be a class act *à la* Coco (who herself had her fair share of failings), great manners, generosity, humility and compassion are just as important as well-cut jackets and designer shoes.

As we all live such busy lives with so many pressures and demands on our time and energy, it can be very easy to forget everyday gestures of thoughtfulness. Focusing on other people rather than only yourself will ensure that you are open to new influences and experiences, help you build better relationships and treating everyone you meet with respect no matter what the context will create a sense of positivity. It will also stop you from becoming too self-involved, something which is endemic in the social media age and very boring for everyone around you.

ELEGANCE IS WHEN THE INSIDE IS AS BEAUTIFUL AS THE OUTSIDE.

15

Stuck in a style rut?
Head to the salon

The cliché of getting a dramatic haircut after
going through heartbreak rings true for a reason.
Changing the frame of your face, whether it's
with a chop or colour, offers a chance of physical
transformation in a way that's impossible outside of
cosmetic surgery. And sometimes, especially when
you are going through shifts in identity created by
new circumstances (breakups, new jobs or moving
home, for example) a new look can help you
psychologically open a new chapter.

In the 1920s, a short haircut symbolized membership of a new sorority of empowered women, or flappers – and there's no doubt that part of the change is in how other people perceive you. Whether you go blonde, opt for a bob or get a fringe cut, you will present a reinvented version of yourself to the world and that in turn can lead to new avenues. Transforming your hair can lead to an increase in confidence (even going through the indulgence of getting yours done can lift your spirits) and a new lease of life if you've been in the doldrums, but it can also be jarring to see a different you staring back in the mirror. If you are nervous to take the plunge, make the change in steps, reaching your new look over time.

How to make an impact with your hair

• The most obvious choice is to go for a drastic change in length. If you have always had billowing tresses, it's a sure-fire way to completely alter the way you feel. If you're keen to take baby steps, start with a trim and go shorter each time until you find yourself with a shorn crop!

• Cutting in a fringe or layers around the face can change your style instantly. While there is a lot of maintenance involved, a fringe adds a quirkier, fashion-forward appeal to all sorts of hair lengths and colours. While it takes time to grow it out, it's a far quicker turnaround than growing a crop back to lengthy tresses.

• Colour. Whether you go from fair to dark, brunette to blonde or experiment with bold red, green or purple, a striking hair colour change can completely transform your looks. While the dramatic change might be appealing, especially when you are lightening your hair from a naturally dark shade, it pays to build the colour up over time. And of course, remember that you'll need to be back in the salon regularly if you want to keep the colour looking permanently polished.

• Wigs, weaves and hairpieces can create a brand new you, in a far more temporary way. Depending on your hair type, you can change colour and cut overnight, then days or weeks later return to your original look. This option will allow you to express yourself in lots of different ways, creating a hair wardrobe for all the sides of your personality.

A WOMAN WHO CUTS HER HAIR IS ABOUT TO CHANGE HER LIFE.

16

Ditch the expectations and the angst will go with them

When you're constantly bombarded with images of media-approved beauty and taught that your value lies in your looks, not your brains, it's inevitable that you will frame yourself as a trophy. Looking good on someone else's arm, in swimwear, as a partner or generally emulating an ideal which pleases others is an ambition which comes complete with agonies and anxieties. It's a full-time job pretending to be something you're not: a chattel, an appendage, a plus one. And while you work so hard to be that thing that you're expected to be, the real you – your voice, your desires, your potential – is smothered and lost in inauthenticity.

As soon as you reorient your goals towards self-development, the whole equation changes. The weight is lifted, the worries relent. We have never had more opportunities to become whomever we want to be, yet paradoxically, we have never been more anxious. The problem is that there are still so many values stitched into our everyday lives which serve to convince people their roles are limited. The answer is simple: stop trying to live by standards you haven't set for yourself and like Coco, set yourself free to fly.

Simple steps to self-care

• Question the status quo. Just because 'everyone' else wants something, doesn't mean it's right for you.

• Status anxiety isn't the same as envy or jealousy. It's when self-worth is linked to how others perceive us. It's an external rather than internal system of validation. If you live your life for other people, it will be hard to find your sense of self.

• The reality is that perceived standards are constantly in flux and hierarchies and values change. The only standards that you should judge yourself by are your own.

HOW MANY CARES ONE LOSES WHEN ONE DECIDES NOT TO BE SOMETHING BUT TO BE SOMEONE.

17

Youth is only one measure of beauty

They say age is just a number, but though it's clear that dividing your life into decades is hopelessly arbitrary, it's disingenuous to pretend that age doesn't make a difference. Rather, accept that every stage has its own appeal which can be equally desirable, and embrace whichever stage you are at.

Although the bloom of youth is undeniably appealing, endlessly chasing after it is neither charming nor irresistible. Aging gracefully is an art which Coco, who was still wearing her bouclé and pearls at 87, totally mastered. Her answer wasn't Botox, it was self-assurance, comfort in her own skin, and a hinterland of life experience and achievement. Now that's charming.

How to re-frame ageing as beautiful

• Remember that 'age appropriate' is a made-up term. There are no rules about what you should be wearing based on your date of birth. If you feel great in a bikini at 90, wear it. If you fancy pink hair at 55, dye it. The ONLY thing that matters is how it makes you feel.

• Value the evolution of your beauty instead of only focusing on the fountain of youth. Being fresh-faced and gorgeous is lovely but remember that being charming and irresistible is even more wonderful. Look forward to getting there.

• Eat well, invest in self-care, enjoy life. These are the keys to ageing happily, so invest the time to find out what makes you tick, rather than lamenting the jeans that don't fit anymore.

"YOU CAN BE GORGEOUS AT THIRTY, CHARMING AT FORTY, AND IRRESISTIBLE FOR THE REST OF YOUR LIFE."

18

Think deeply, but laugh loudly too

The opportunity for 24-hour news consumption means that world events, often involving bad news, are inescapable. While engaging in the issues of the day will always be fundamentally important, allowing them to overwhelm you and your happiness serves no one. Keeping light-hearted, at least in some element of your personal life, is an important safety valve.

Coco's ideas and beliefs were profound in that they challenged the prevailing order of the day, especially in terms of the role of women. But she always kept wit on her side, even on the most serious of topics. She knew the value of merriment, even if it were only to sugar the pill of her more rebellious maxims. Funny people have been shown to be happier, healthier and less stressed – something we can all aspire to.

YOU LIVE BUT ONCE; YOU MIGHT AS WELL BE AMUSING.

19

There's more to life than materialism (but you can still treat yourself)

Taking joy in beauty, be it found in the natural world or in art, is free for all. Finding contentment in love, whether it be the love of a partner, child or friend, remains priceless. Loneliness or disenchantment cannot be cured through buying things and no matter how much money you have, you can still live a life bereft of the only gifts that truly matter.

However, while the most important things in life aren't Chanel 2.55s or strings of pearls (or cars, luxury homes or expensive five-star holidays, or whatever floats your boat), that doesn't mean they can't have a deeper value. This is particularly true when they symbolize an achievement or an investment in yourself. Buying a designer handbag with your first paycheck after a promotion, for example, is something which can feel incredibly empowering, because it's a choice you have made exclusively yourself and will always represent your dedication and a moment of personal success. Owning handmade, iconic pieces of design, which you can pass on to the next generation is the exact opposite of throwaway fashion and as a result is not going to be cheap. But that is not the same as being overpriced. Be wise about your investments: always prioritize the things that don't cost a thing, but when you're spending, make sure it will stand the test of time.

"

THE BEST THINGS IN LIFE ARE FREE. THE SECOND-BEST THINGS ARE VERY, VERY EXPENSIVE.

"

20

There's no such thing as new style

If Coco Chanel, one of the most original and revolutionary designers of all time, can admit to taking references from the past, then we can be pretty sure that there's no such thing as a totally new idea. We all grow up with a certain prism on the world, which applies to both our ideas and aesthetic style. Added to all sorts of other influences, this creates what Mark Twain described as a 'mental kaleidoscope' which we turn to create new combinations.

Coco Chanel wasn't the first woman in history to wear a black dress. Or a skirt suit. Or wear pearls. Nor did she profess to be such. Her aim was always to take old ideas and styles – in her case often from menswear and utility wear – and reimagine them for new uses and new ways to wear them. The lesson is that you can look to the past for inspiration, but for a style renaissance, you need a fresh take on a look, rather than a carbon copy.

How to make the old feel new

• Nearly every designer and buyer for high street stores go 'shopping' in vintage stores or their own archive to find inspiration for new styles. You can take that principle and run with it on an individual level, saving money and ensuring that your pieces are entirely unique.

• With vintage and second-hand, you never want to wear the look head to toe. Say you find a wonderful 70s-style evening dress, you don't buy the platforms and oversized hat to match, instead go for a modern kitten heel mule and black nylon mini tote.

• While physical vintage shops are great, there are amazing vintage and second-hand options online, too. With a tailor on hand, you can make sure that the fit is adjusted to more modern tastes as well as your figure.

ONLY THOSE WITH NO MEMORY INSIST ON THEIR ORIGINALITY.

21

Everyone has the potential to fly

Some people are naturally confident and possessing self-assurance in their own worth isn't something they have to work at. For the vast majority, however, self-esteem is forged and melded through experience, over years of life lived, obstacles overcome and achievements under the belt. Instead of a 'fake it 'til you make it' version of confidence, Coco suggests that your job isn't to pretend you have something that you don't, but to clear the path for real personal growth.

The problem with mimicking self-belief is that you open yourself up to the anxieties of imposter syndrome. Constantly feeling like you are going to be found out can undermine all aspects of your life and ironically end up making you feel less confident. But Coco's idea of ensuring you don't stand in the way of your own future is something which many of us could feel more comfortable observing. It's never too late to find yourself, start again or take up something new. Life is one long lesson, you owe it to yourself to keep learning how to fly.

IF YOU WERE BORN WITHOUT WINGS, DO NOTHING TO PREVENT THEM FROM GROWING.

22

Fashion is more than the clothes we wear

Fashion can provide you with the armour to face the day, but it's also worth considering how design – and beauty – is more than just skin-deep superficiality. Coco understood that the mastery of adornment was a skill, requiring knowledge and discipline rather than vapid narcissism. What you wear is also a canvas for self-expression, so the better you know yourself, the more accurately you will be able to reflect your identity through what you wear. In that sense, fashion is like a language used to communicate a host of messages about how you want the world to understand you.

It would be disingenuous to suggest that physical beauty doesn't make a difference – 'pretty privilege' can have a huge impact on your life opportunities. As long as social standards keep the definition of that beauty narrow, the vast majority of us are likely to feel we fall short. While there are multibillion dollar businesses whose bottom lines rely on us striving towards one narrow standard, Coco always knew that true style was a far broader church. Her belief was that beauty comes from knowing yourself and using fashion to convey your true essence – meaning whatever your genetic code, you have the right to use your own brand of beauty to achieve your personal goals.

Use fashion to get ahead

• Fashion can help you wield power and influence, just look at the wardrobes of confident and powerful women from Michelle Obama to Oprah Winfrey.

• Beautifully tailored clothing will always impress, but it's not necessarily the expense that matters, more how confidently you carry yourself in those clothes.

• For a boost of confidence, try an interesting styling twist. For example, take a simple jeans and blazer combination – add a wide belt over the blazer and a silk scarf and you suddenly have something creative and individual.

• While power dressing used to mean skirt suits and shoulder pads, today a sharply cut shift dress or an elegant tuxedo suit are great options. However, true authority comes from feeling like your most empowered self, so if that's in cords and a Breton, all power to you.

ADORNMENT, WHAT A SCIENCE! BEAUTY, WHAT A WEAPON!

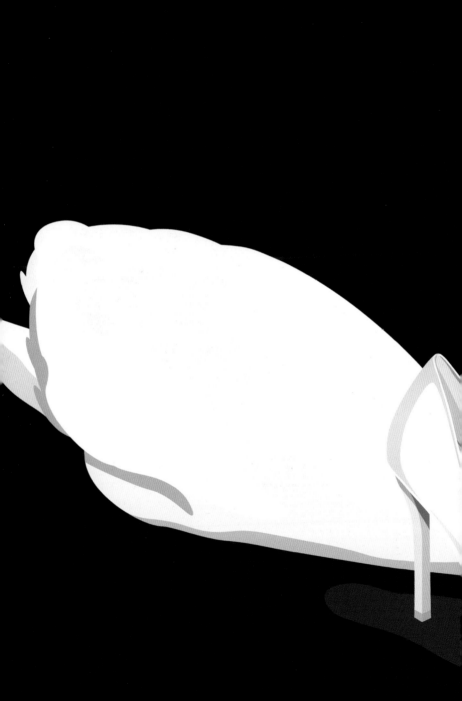

23

Learn to live outside the box

Coco Chanel was at once both an elegant lady and a vivacious rebel. She pushed the boundaries of respectability throughout her life, living through an age in which impropriety amongst women could be swiftly punished. She was a mistress and a mischief maker, but she also designed some of the most undeniably classy products of all time. Coco knew the rules, but she also didn't hesitate to break them.

While our sense of morality may have become more tolerant and less misogynistic, who hasn't felt the strictures of society stifle their originality? Convention and accepted ideals of how to live can not only make you believe that you have failed, but also can obscure your true lane. To be absolutely fabulous, you have to find the confidence to step outside the norm and avoid the lemming-like procession through life's milestones. And if you can do that with class, you'll be well on the path that Coco paved.

Use your style to break the rules with class

• Coco challenged the role of women in society by dressing in outfits inspired by menswear, allowing for more movement and participation in spheres of life which were once limited to men only. Whether you make new connections through expressing yourself on social media or use fashion to communicate your self-confidence to get a job, aesthetics can open closed doors in many different ways.

• If you do want to rebel against the norms of the people around you, remember to be respectful in the way you communicate it. There are no worse or better ways to live, and you should never judge other people's choices in life – they are on their own journey as you are on yours. It's never classy to put anyone else's lifestyle down.

" A GIRL SHOULD BE TWO THINGS: CLASSY AND FABULOUS. "

24

Wear your 'revenge wardrobe' 365 days a year

It's the kind of thing you have anxiety daydreams about: on the only day you don't shower, your hair is stuck to your forehead and your outfit is all wrong, you bump into your ex. Or your former colleague who stabbed you in the back. Or someone from school who made your life hell. While no-one is saying that you have to dress to the nines every single day of your life just in case you bump into your nemesis, taking the time to choose something that makes you feel good can give you that 'take on the world' boost, no matter what the day might bring.

What Coco suggests is harnessing the motivation to help turbo-charge your sartorial prowess. If you imagine the look on your adversary's face when they clock your strong and confident vibe, it can certainly help you up the ante and make the effort for yourself. While forgiveness may be the best revenge, using fashion to help you feel the most confident version of you comes a close second.

Three ways to supercharge your staples

1. Build a collection of belts
One of the most underrated accessories, the belt can add polish to jeans and casual separates, define your silhouette and literally pull an outfit together. Requiring minimum effort and thought, a great belt will immediately elevate your look.

2. Same shirt, different colour
If you find yourself constantly reaching for the same things – a linen shirt or a silk slip for example, never hesitate to

3. Invest in outerwear
If you live in a country with long winters, for several months of the year the only thing most people will see you wearing is your coat. It's therefore the most important item in your wardrobe, and as such where a sizeable chunk of your wardrobe budget should go. In warmer climes, go for beautiful cashmere cardigans if budget allows, and printed shawls for chillier days and evenings.

DRESS LIKE YOU ARE GOING TO MEET YOUR WORST ENEMY TODAY.

25

Audacity and adventure are always attractive assets

Coco certainly had a devil-may-care attitude to dressing, and she pleased herself with abandon, whether it was by cutting her hair into a gamine crop or wearing layers of costume jewellery. That sense of liberty and independence will always be appealing, because who doesn't want the confidence to live their life and dress in a way which suits their own compass rather than comply with the rules?

Rebels with or without a cause are alluring simply because breaking with tradition is exciting and provides a welcome break from 'same old, same old'. It is far easier to mindlessly do exactly what everyone else does, wearing the same brands and the same trends in a bid to either fit in or be accepted than it is to rock the boat and try something new. Coco's idea of freedom also encompasses comfort and ease – the freedom to do anything in the clothes you are wearing, unhampered by restrictive cuts or heavy hemlines.

How to dress with a sense of freedom

• Feeling free in your clothing can operate on several levels. You can feel free when you are dressing most like yourself, unconstrained by social or cultural values and confident in your own look.

• Think about cut and fit. No-one feels free in a size-too-small dress pulling at the seams, or a skirt that edges just that bit too short, or, the very worst, shoes that absolutely don't fit. Donate every piece of clothing that has ever made you feel encumbered, because they will never be stylish on you.

• Dressing with freedom is the same as dressing without a care about what anyone thinks about your outfit. As long as you like it, it's wonderful. Finding that freedom from judgement is one of the most important steps in discovering your own innate sense of style.

66

A SENSE
OF FREEDOM
IS ALWAYS
STYLISH.

99

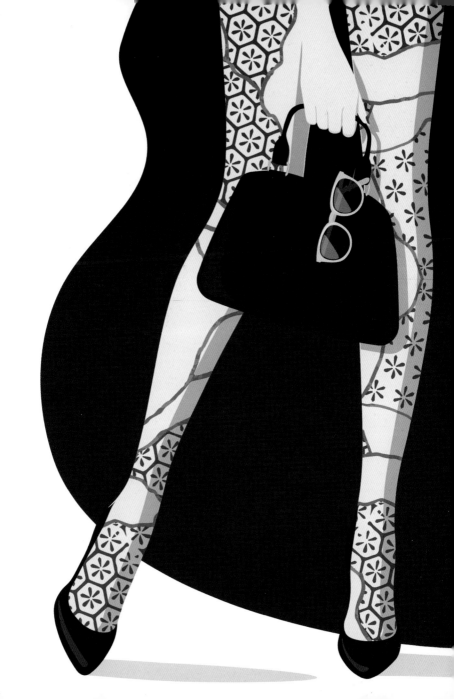

26

Embrace the markers of your difference

Revelling in both her strengths and weaknesses, Coco implicitly understood that her value came from the ways in which she wasn't just another well-dressed woman. What set her apart was courage, panache, conviction and wit, the combination of which has made her probably the most famous fashion designer of all time, an icon whose words still reverberate nearly 140 years after she was born. There will never be another Coco, she will never be eclipsed, and her shadow will remain long, simply because she was one of a kind.

While not all of us may find ourselves in history books, the secret to shining so bright is based on the celebration – and acceptance – of our own uniqueness. Look to the Japanese art of *kintsugi*, which involves repairing broken pottery with lacquer mixed with gold or silver – for an inspiring take on celebrating imperfections rather than disguising them. It may also help to remember that no meaningful relationships can be formed when you can't be your authentic self. Until you feel confident with your warts and all, you'll find it all but impossible to make true connections.

"

**IN ORDER
TO BE
IRREPLACEABLE,
ONE MUST
ALWAYS BE
DIFFERENT.**

"

27

Choose your scent wisely as it offers a lasting memory

In 1921, Coco created her first perfume, Chanel N° 5. It was the first fragrance ever to be named after a designer and was accompanied by her lucky number five. Back in the 1920s, well-to-do women only wore subtle floral scents, with the headier aromas of musk and jasmine associated with the *demi-monde*, women on the fringes of respectable society. N° 5 changed all of that, with its complex composition of florals and woody fragrances, created for the modern, more independent flapper – a scent which is intoxicating, sensual, but also somewhat scandalous. Today Chanel N° 5 is arguably the world's most iconic perfume and it made Coco the richest woman in the world.

For Coco, perfume was part of the dress code, and the only accessory which left an indelible memory. Without it, she believed a woman wasn't fully dressed. When choosing your perfume, look for something which reflects how you wish to be perceived and one that can work as an olfactory signature – enabling you to convey a message without ever having to say anything. Take your time to experiment with perfumes and when you are trialling each fragrance, allow it to develop on your skin, so you can smell the different 'notes' or layers of aromas. A signature scent isn't an impulse purchase, so bide your time, try lots of perfumiers and never buy a perfume because of its bottle – however beautiful it might be.

Which notes create your signature scent?

Hesperidia: fresh, citrusy scents for a cheerful, youthful perfume. Look for notes of lemon, bergamot, orange or grapefruit.

Chypre: intense and characterful, these scents are charismatic and impactful. Seek out note mixtures of jasmine, rose and patchouli.

Floral: offering a vast range of scents, from powdery to spicy florals, there are floral notes for every personality. Try lily, ylang ylang, iris and orange blossom for a timeless, feminine fragrance.

Amber: originally created from highly prized raw materials from the East, the amber family of fragrances are sensual, earthy and warm. Musk, myrrh, frankincense and vanilla all fall under the amber umbrella

Woody: most often attributed to masculine scents, woody fragrances have become increasingly unisex and are a great choice for a sexy, adventurous perfume. Think cedar, sandalwood, vetiver and cypress.

Aromatic: also known as the *fougère*, or fern family, these scents again are usually featured in men's fragrances, with a clean freshness or spiciness being the main characteristics. Combining sage, rosemary, cumin and lavender, it's a great choice for natural power.

NO ELEGANCE IS POSSIBLE WITHOUT PERFUME. IT IS THE UNSEEN, UNFORGETTABLE, ULTIMATE ACCESSORY.

28

How it feels is as important as how it looks

If you have to adjust the waistband, hobble in shoes, constantly pull down your hem, breathe in or avoid all food or drink to wear a garment, it is not a luxury experience, however expensive the price tag may have been. Part of luxury fashion is the way it makes you feel to wear it and that is completely negated if you're not comfy, too.

While it's also always great to experiment, when you're spending a luxury sum of money, it's not the time to go too far outside of your comfort zone. While the sales might seem like a good opportunity to nab a piece by your favourite brand, always make sure it's a piece you will feel comfortable wearing in your actual life (rather than the fantasy one on board a super yacht or partying in a private members club). However beautiful that be-feathered, be-ruffled, be-sequined floor length gown might be, if it's going to hang unworn in your wardrobe from now until the end of time, it's no bargain.

Before you remove the tags from a new purchase …

• Sit down on a chair or bench to make sure the rise isn't too short in jeans or trousers, or the waistline becomes uncomfortably tight.

• With deep necklines, move around and take a seat to ensure that they don't fall too far forward.

• Pay attention to the lining – silks, satins and cotton, yes. Synthetic linings will do you zero favours.

• Now we're on to fabric, breathable is where you want to go. Cotton and wool allow moisture to escape while polyester will trap your sweat and probably make you sweat even more. That is not a luxury experience.

• Beware of vanity sizing and remember that measurements of certain sizes can vary from brand to brand. Make a rule to try on two sizes of anything you are interested in buying.

LUXURY MUST BE COMFORTABLE, OTHERWISE IT IS NOT LUXURY.

29

Think big: never let other people's ideas limit you

Born in a poorhouse to a laundrywoman and street vendor, at the age of 11, and after the death of her mother, Coco was placed in an orphanage. Coming from such an underprivileged background without any protectors, the opportunities for a girl like Coco at the end of the 19th century were far from dazzling. But that didn't stop her from becoming the richest woman in the world and an icon of fashion history. It was Coco's charisma and striking sense of style, as well as her business sense, which helped catapult her life into the stratosphere; it was also her survival instinct and stubborn resilience. No matter what the world threw at her, she remained focused on the life she had dreamt of and never let any setbacks stop her in her tracks.

While today women of all backgrounds enjoy broader opportunities with fewer barriers against advancement and success, there are still countless hurdles and prejudices to overcome for many. Self belief is your ally in turning the roles that people might assume you will fill upside down, as well as the understanding that there is no straight path to the life you wish to live. Like Coco, you will have to ruffle some feathers and break some rules along the way, but believing in the possibilities is the first step towards creating a life far beyond the confines of the one you were born into. It takes luck, tenacity and a dogged determination to manifest a new destiny, so just like Coco, never give up.

MY LIFE DIDN'T PLEASE ME, SO I CREATED MY LIFE.

30

Wear clothes for living by your own rules

Coco's first and most important rule would be that there are no rules when it comes to thinking for yourself. If you don't agree with everyone else, say so; if you don't love a certain look or trend, feel no pressure to follow the sartorial crowd.

What you wear outside of the house is one of the ways you can express to the world who you are – out loud. It's both challenging and liberating to break off from the fashion pack, especially if you have become used to blending into your tribe. It can also take bravery to go your own way, especially if you are still finding your own voice, but fashion is an amazing vehicle for experimenting with different versions of the person you might one day want to be.

There is nothing better for creating confidence than being 100% true to yourself, whether that's in your opinions on the biggest issues of the day or in wearing exactly what you like, whether or not it's in vogue. Having the courage of your convictions is perennially chic.

Want to step out of your style pack?

Try these tricks and repeat the mantra: "It is not my job to please other people."

• Start with an informal occasion to introduce pieces which appeal to you, whether it's putting together a more minimalist look or bringing print and colour into your outfits.

• Spend time trying on the pieces you love in your wardrobe. Try styling them in new ways that make you feel original and inspired.

• Feel confident before you leave the house and hold on to that feeling as best you can.

" THE MOST COURAGEOUS ACT IS STILL TO THINK FOR YOURSELF. ALOUD. "

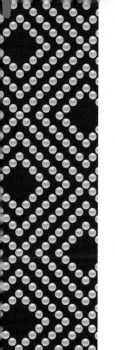

**ILLUSTRATED BY
CAROLINA MELIS**

**WRITTEN BY
KATHERINE ORMEROD**

EDITED BY JOCELYN NORBURY

COVER DESIGNED BY ANGIE ALLISON

DESIGNED BY ZOE BRADLEY

First published in Great Britain in 2022 by LOM ART,
an imprint of Michael O'Mara Books Limited,
9 Lion Yard, Tremadoc Road, London SW4 7NQ

 www.mombooks.com/lom

 Michael O'Mara Books

 @OMaraBooks

 @lomartbooks

Copyright © Michael O'Mara Books Limited 2022

All rights reserved.

No part of this book may be reproduced, stored in a retrieval system, or transmitted in
any form or by any means, without the prior permission in writing of the publisher, nor be
otherwise circulated in any form of binding or cover other than that in which it is published
and without a similar condition including this condition being imposed on the subsequent purchaser.

A CIP catalogue record for this book is available from the British Library.

ISBN: 978-1-912785-63-6

10 9 8 7 6 5 4 3 2 1

This book was printed in China.